Spirit Level

Spirit Level

Marcelle Freiman

PUNCHER & WATTMANN

First published in 2021
Published by Puncher and Wattmann
PO Box 279
Waratah NSW 2298

http://www.puncherandwattmann.com
puncherandwattmann@bigpond.com

ISBN   9781922571144

Cover design and typesetting by Morgan Arnett
Printed by Lightning Source International

Contents

II.

'The world not as it was, or as
we were, but as we find ourselves
again in its presence…'

David Malouf,
'À la Recherche,' *An Open Book*, 2018

I.

Still

there is a stillness I require
no rain drumming the surfaces of things.
now, there is no quiescent water
rather a dry crackle of grasses, a sunset in Africa
yellow-brown and moving soft as hair.
only the child's eye can see
a memory like this. a making of time.
here, there is nothing in your eyes
that can take me back there –
though I want those traces of past
where every stone turns for me
as the line grows shorter. the stillness
I seek is not darkness: it is the shimmer
of red at the centre of the throat
of a leather-faced monkey calling across acacias,
a heart-muscle pink as flamingos against
a mirror of russet plains.
the thrum of rain on the roof returns.
times of dislocation – each sense
a feeler reaching for the light

Crickets

Johannesburg, 1956

Walking home from school
the roads hard-edged
brick yellow houses, tile and corrugated iron
a grey dog barking on a chain.

Dusty smell, gardens unwatered
said 'no-one's home', the dryness
could bend me like a bow —

but round a corner on 12th Avenue
nannies' voices like bells
the afternoon their resting time,
the green-brown crickets
began to grind their legs together
in bottle-brush up against the fence,
purple velvet moth-dust all down the street.

A hole in the sky of memory opens
unlocks a reach of gravel pale as resin —
jacarandas stand a silent choir
crickets' vibrato washing the stones.

Campbell Street Night c. 1960

From my bed at night, a chorus of frogs
the moon behind trees. early morning
grind of gears, buses on the main highway
beyond suburban rooftops. the crunch
of a spade turning soil, a gardener
first awake before heat rises from the lawn –
our house. just a few miles away
other lives beating, corrugated shanties,
the township beyond the highway:
the same sky, the same sunlit morning.

Another night, different as an emblem –
through bedroom-window bars
heard a man crying out – over and over
the street outside reverberated
the moonlit sky, frog-song silenced:
the man sprawled on the tarred road,
his mangled bicycle. unable to move
his legs, bled a pool on the bitumen,
the sharpened spoke of a bicycle wheel
spearing his back, pitched from the curve
of his spine as he lay on the road,
the siren piercing the street-lit night.

Country of my birth – written 27 June 2013

1.
Today Nelson Mandela is ailing
    in a Pretoria hospital
    in the land I fled in 1977
          anxious as a *Duiker*.

How did I love (hate) a country
       where I knew so much silence?

In blank surfaces of days
did not hear

       his voice
       his fugitive life, the Boksburg strikes
       (where my grandparents lived) of May 1961,
       his words that rang across
       the courtroom of his truth
       in 1962
       were Treason in the *Sunday Times*,
whispers
    overheard at home – of 'Rivonia'

names splintered the night,
my father at the table with a whisky: something
about Braam Fischer – Dad knew of his arrest.

       I was thirteen in 1964
       skinny, growing,
       knew nothing
of the people's words
from rooftops, stations, sidings,
    factories –

my ears stoppered:
then whispers would turn to more –
bold teacher taught high-school girls our history,
while censors rained fear on us –

seven years later in 1971 at nineteen, truth would out
                    white protests, students:

the blue-uniformed policeman
brown leather holster revolvered
me in revolving door,
between action and
                    fear –
                        snatched from
        my hands the Roneo leaflets
                    black ink still damp
                    stains on my fingers.

But we marched our placards down Commissioner Street,
law student boyfriend protective: 'If the cops come, run'
                    and we ran –
                            then
heard of leaders, writers, slipped in showers they said
            in John Vorster Square
or fell from windows,
brothers, students arrested at university gates
                released on the Vice-Chancellor's plea, police
                promises not to record 'crimes' of protest
                                    were betrayed
                                    we later discovered –

and all white boys had to do their time, army conscripts
at eighteen to fight for
                on behalf of
                apartheid

2.

All those intractable years 1963 to 1982
     Mandela in prison
          the white dust of Robben Island's
          quarries
               in his lungs,
     he knew he was right,
     held to what was
       right:

the country made him wrong
     the years took his freedom, he lived on
     black prisoner's meagre diet, with hard labour.

The country took so many,
held them servile,
cut back and low
          like young trees –
myth of Bantu Education, the Pass Laws
     refusing residence
     land
     family –
until the people could not count
     what was stolen
     each day toiling down
     mines, in factories –

     (Can childhood draw blame?)
     I had no language
          for the lost –
we lived in white houses of difference,
and if my father could bribe the
          Pass Office
          bureaucrat

for Albert our gardener from Mozambique
        to stay
        to work
        to grow our garden with flowers,
        spread topsoil on our green lawn and
        not be deported, despite having no Pass –
a drop in an ocean
        his kindness –
my father

             worked the system

and kept it quiet – the whispered names,
             the safe houses of the 1960s
        for friends in banished parties
        African National Congress, South African Communist Party –

nobody talking:
the stories have gone with my father
    to Johannesburg's West Park Cemetery.

        A country of tawny winter grass
        and dust blowing from mine dumps,
        dry eucalyptus trees along
             a road
             where ragged workers
             tramped after fourteen-hour days,
where difference meant gunshots in
        the backs of schoolchildren
             in Soweto June 1976
        and more strikes that stopped everything,
        so much (hope and) fear, it tasted bitter –

and the men who spoke truth
            still sat on bunks in prison cells
            made plans for their future country,
wrote on scraps of paper.

3.
I am born of a country of misery, its
        scales tipped wildly
                        for too many years –

        from its ashes and punctured oil-drum heaters,
        from fingerless gloves in Highveld
                        winter frost at dawn,
        from languages I never learned,
            my brain bleached by other
        chronicles of difference –

        to the hills of Xhosaland in the Transkei
                from which ascended this bird of hope
                        and then forgiveness
                (how could this happen?)
                        his presence
                        a burning star in a country gone wrong
                        where ash and plastic litter township streets,
                        Diepsloot, Alexandria –
                        the harshness goes on, he is loved:

        no electricity in concrete rooms,
        candles flicker in the night.

Their Soles

The soles of her feet when she
sits on the sand
by the breakwater, watching over
      the white boy in his sunhat
      digging, building castles.

The soles of her (her?) feet
crossed over, poked from beneath
the blanket – she sleeps on
a pallet on the floor of
the room she shares with
ten other people.

The nape of her neck, her
white *doek* knotted there
as she prays on the
beach with her church group.

The brown nape of his neck (the young man),
shirt loose to receive the ocean
waves on wide Muizenberg
beach, his baptism.
His white shirt (in the water)
his white shroud as the
waves turn him over
and over.

The soles of his feet (the
white boy?) flat and sinking
in soft sand, the shallow
waves breaking.

Their bare feet in the
sand as they sing,
a prayer circle, their white
robes (the men).

The soles of his feet (the young man)
a room with an iron chair,
the burn-holes, bleeding scorched skin —

the soles of their feet
pale, hardened:
        soft as my untouched palm.

The Dam

1.
November 1959, holidays on the smallholding where
      my grandparents lived, on the road in Klipfontein, Boksburg,
           their general store –
gold-seam lying deep beneath flat country,
horizon of mine dump tailings, plots of straw-coloured grassland,
      silver poplars along the straight road.

A summer day going swimming, we walked across
      the yellow *veld*, towels rolled under our arms,
           treading the sandy path through the orchard,
the light squinty: flitter of shadows and sunlight,
Highveld noon, the zizz of flies, cricket rasp in the faded grass –
      the horse in next-door's field blowing through its nostrils,
flapping its lips in the blaze of sun, the crack and scuffle
      of our sandals on stony gravel.

The dam, a concrete reservoir fed water to the house and orchard,
      loomed ahead, a squat cylinder at the end of the paddock –
soon we were climbing – onto the narrow wall, legs straddling
      then over, my feet like little whitish paddles.
In the midday glare tadpoles bumped in rows,
      their heads a ring of beads on the wall's edge,
a circle of light surrounding the watery darkness:
holding the ladder, I backed in, heels pressed,
      toes gripping the sludgy coating.

Above our heads the windpump clanked as the wind changed direction,
      its tailfin a sail, blades turning lazy and squeaking:
my brother calling out explained how the pump-shaft
      pulled water from the dark ground aquifers below.

We hovered, the water tasting of metal and rock,
          the boys splashed, ducking under, then up shouting
while I pushed out from the mossy wall, doggie-paddling –
          clouds of itchy dust came down from the plane trees,
          yellow flecks sprinkling the surface:
with tadpoles and slime of frogspawn we made trails,
          small circles in the water.

I see us now as if from above, our tiny tracks
sunlit splashes marking an hour in an afternoon, our kicks footprints
          in a timespan, evanescent spray-puffs in the heat of day.
Ducking my face, open-eyed – the floor thick-layered silt and mud,
          the cold through my hair, swimsuit billowing,
          my scurries muddying the sediment, drifting it up,
turned the water murky brown so I could no longer see –
          hurrying back to the concrete wall,
                    the sharp rusty peel of the ladder,
          glad to hear the clank of the wind pump overhead.

Then walking home, chatter and peach trees,
                    thrum of bees, a shuddering horse –
          and in early afternoon heat
          the repeated thwack and chop
of Jacob's mattock as he swung then hit against the hard ground
          by the *mielie* patch behind the house –
because this story is also about Jacob,
his English name (I don't remember any other),
          who taught me to greet *dumela* in Sotho,
          who helped me to see which side of the scale was mine.

2.
Beyond fence palings at the garden boundary,
          a low brick building, corrugated iron roof,
chicken-wire pens, a stand of eucalyptus trees:

a row of rooms with a concrete stoop, Jacob's wife scooping water
        with a tin-can from a bucket,
                the run-off making runnels in the dust.

Jacob was years with my grandparents: lived in those rooms
                with his family, worked in their store
        along the road that led to the clay quarry:
that summer he taught me how to fill
        and clean-fold brown paper packets,
                then weigh-check using the scales on the store-room bench:
I remember the wrinkling of his eyes, how he'd lean in to my height
        our faces close – I'd match his eye-line with my own,
the brass bowl of the scale, the way we dropped the heavy weights
        on the balancing rod, iron wedges and small brass discs
                thin as pennies, then tipped in more
– sugar, *stamp-mielies*, quarter-pound, half-pound –
                the weight of each packet precise.

The memory now a flat bubble in a spirit level measure in time –
        when the slow goods-train came by at noon each day
on its way from the quarry to the brickworks, then again at night:
        I can still hear the dogs barking
        in answer to the faraway echo of the whistle and chuff
as I lay in my bed in the house: night-time, a grid of connections –
        my brothers, my grandparents, Jacob and the dogs close-by.

3.
Years later, I stepped from my car near a Sydney park – cut loose
        from those ties that had meshed my life
        in that hard country where things could grow:
ties like torn mosquito netting on a window –
                my frayed, white memory:
        I would not see Jacob's years unfold,
        his children ground to their core by apartheid.

The tattered, unfinished fabric I trailed across the Indian Ocean
        to this shore: its cords had sunk to the bottom
        imperceptible as tiny hairline cracks
or mottled patterns marbling a bone: scars that itch and ache
        each time I hear the rub of crickets on summer afternoons –

that day at Watsons Bay by a stand of ti-tree bushes and eucalyptus,
        in a split-second stepping – something opened –
like a crack in the shell of the day – as if in a rush of feathers
            flared past my head –
        a tremor in the air shot through from the feldspar and quartz
of the sandstone rocks in this Sydney park
        on the rim of the harbour I was held to
        by gravity, my heart pumping –
the sudden flash shook me: like a small weight dropping to a scale
        it intimated more – that there was more to everything:
            the warm afternoon layered
infinitely more than itself, a plenitude, stratified
        and deep as the shelf of rock I was standing on,
        a chance in the weave of that day (any day) to take hold
look again, no matter the grit in my eyes,
for rust-coloured rainwater and a circular dam,
        the blades turning, cranking a water pump,
        cold water beneath the surface of hard country.

Greyhounds – on the plots

Fridays with Jacob:
the fence round the compound,
mine-dumps on the horizon, a space of chicken sheds,
a brick room where greyhound pups
were silver backed and frisky when you entered:
the dogs he bred for racing, prized and illegal,
trained along the fence. I was eight,
ours a friendship – he'd lift me
to the wagon's bench made
from fence-palings rubbed smooth,
then horse-drawn we'd leave
the general store, deliver to farmers
living on the plots and collect
the order money before Friday pubs were opened:
flat, dun country, the shunting train from the quarry,
greyhound bitch back in the wagon tray,
bags of *stamp-mielies* for Viljoen's workers,
the smell of yeast in Jacob's pocket
for the local shebeen queen's son.

Shadow Play

On the wall above the wardrobe in our room,
the frieze my mother sewed on linen:
appliquéd sheep, a farmer's wife,
embroidered stitches on her apron.

*

Black, white, sepia landscapes,
each one a fragment –
her white coral necklace,
earrings, green eyes, young snapshot
with cigarette on the veranda –
her light shaded in facets:
smiling, in shorts with a bottle of Coke –
or sewing rickrack on dresses she made for me.

*

Behind a garage door
with my brother we two convince
with sweets the neighbour's daughter
to take off her clothes. We were trouble
in our hidden play.

*

Suburban fences were our boundaries:
walls disintegrate with distance,
memories plunge into grainy film –
dad's super-eight crackling like static:
the months sewing that frieze,
it draped our dreams at night –
a stitch, a tapestry – come, then gone.

Aloe

Johannesburg 2010

Paper fish in the window of the old house
orange black stripes against the glass
curtains drawn wide open,
flickers of light, small shadows dancing –
children now live in this house:

what happened to our lives here –
back then, our father turning
slowly bent broken with illness,
our mother in the dark
wanting non-life – it seemed –
no longer loving the birds
feasting on blossoms of flowering peach,
the bounty of avocadoes on dark green branches?

Years earlier, she looked out from the window seat,
that aloe she'd planted in the garden:
tough-leaved, thorns protecting
edges mottled white and green –
all winter Cape robins came to suck insects
and nectar from tubular clusters
rising high and vertical from thorny calyx –
orange flames set against the Highveld grass,
the frosts each night turned the grass-blades white –
the birds' frenzied feeding,
their pitched cries returning each year,
pitting the late afternoons.

Poinsettias

We know them best in warm summer light
against a North brick wall,
leafy red bracts flame bright
wheels turning their faces to the sun —
they could be sharp as a heart turned sour,
always it seemed they were the only flowers
without infolded petals,
their waxy yellow clusters
tough, uncertain hearts —
yet their scarlet could open a woman's tongue
to the tug and passion she knows well.

These, from the garden, in a plain brown vase,
tinted with brown ochre and the tired curve
of being too long in this world,
their bent necks drooped dry as a cheek
resting on a cool, white sheet,
petal-bracts bent back, showing
what an enduring face has hidden:
shadows of leaf-dry skin.

Brave Face

A small flame in the storm
this flutter each day and night –
skin loosens, joints tighten to drums
in the light before daybreak
the road seems narrow.
Some days, feathers moult the wooden floor,
eyes lighter, voice a whisper, a heart
opens wide the ink-prints of its pages.

On the path outside a bird on papery grass,
dead feathers limp, still glossed, blue-black
not yet stiffening – this dry late-winter afternoon
I think of tenacity, of dust.

Seven Ways of Mourning

Your name bends out of reach,
        the final spike shreds the skin
of my remembering.

Engraved on stone, words
        tell: they came to this country
they lived here, and died.

To show you scarlet
        bougainvillea in autumn –
your dark hound refused it.

Throw waiting hours
        down like coins in black water:
lost, they shake like stars.

The name rests, a bench
        by the sea: fingertip touch
on each breaking wave.

If everything ran
        out, each vessel empty, clean,
would muscle turn to stone?

Forgetting is like
        light on sharp edged fences,
clears spaces between.

The Mother Poems

1. Passport

My mother sits in her armchair – by her side
photographs and a document assembled in a frame:
1931 a Lithuanian passport: the handwritten words identify
my grandmother Chana b.1903 and Mina b.1926.
Alongside, a snapshot in a forest of birches –
a satchel on her shoulder, the child looks straight at the camera,
her heart-shaped face, a half-smile,
the shine of a clear lake through the trees.
The paper document steered them to South Africa,
to her waiting father, my grandfather (bookkeeper
and Yiddish writer) – he'd worked three years in a store
by the Kimberley diamond diggings
in this thornbush stony country called Free State,
sent money for their passage from Hamburg in the north
towards the southern sun.

More than nine decades inhabit this room –
in her chair, her forehead dented from surgery,
her body abundant with the traces of her life,
tenacious as imprint folds of the document in the frame,
the arc from childhood to full vessel that carried my own.

2. Irises and Thorn

I walk in the gardens, winter sun on brittle grass,
a lake rimmed with bulrushes – a mother duck launches,
her ducklings follow, fuzzy tails leaving ripples
the light catching droplets shaken from feathers.
A group of irises by the edge of a pathway
their purple tissue-paper tongues lit with yellow –
the bright centres echo the heart-shaped head-dress
of my mother's wedding veil the day she married my father,
sewed fresh sweet-peas to a gauzed frame, with foliage
to match the splendid green of her eyes.

A red-leafed bush with berries attracts weaver birds and sparrows,
pushes between pelindaba rocks, glows in the dun-brown garden.
Close by, a great thorn-bush looms bare over the walkway,
grid-like shadows of silver branches, thorns inches long
crown my eye-line – I remember at fourteen
one of these thorns sunk deep in the sole of my foot –
could not know then in my involuntary cry
how the strength of my grandmother would not be enough
to heal the sharpness my mother's mind would bear.

3. Wires

My mother's life is wide, plumbed deep and unreachable
for a daughter pinning a map of inheritance
with stories she told me: her mother Chana taught languages,
learned English those first months in this city,
walked up Doornfontein Hill from the boarding house
each week to her lessons, holding her daughter's hand,
for ten years, wrote letters in Yiddish to her mother
in Lithuania – then the notice from the Red Cross came –
her mother Sara, and her sister, were gone.
In 1945, we learned much later, the family perished
in the forest bordering their shtetl of Simnas – an entire town:
a myriad moth wings echoed unmarked graves,
shade and light of birches in Lithuanian June – the same light
that shone in a four-year old's eyes gazing at a camera lens
where a lake glinted through the trees.

In the south, the news would sink Chana, her body punched inward,
it shadowed her mind for a long time: no language
to speak the engulfing darkness – then
she would go on, weaving threads of connection
holding each tradition, lighting candles on Shabbos
remembering the Shoah, candles wrapped in black cloth – reciting
Yizkor prayers on the women's balcony on Yom Kippur
as her mother had done, her eyes on the number tattooed
on the forearm of a woman in the next row
where a sleeve had fallen back.

Through wordless nights, with steel wires
tying her to family, she made new life in the sun – my mother
a proof of it: snapshot of a young nursery-school teacher
wild-haired and free at eighteen.
Ambiguous, the losses of family not spoken,

the traces would ripple close to the frames
of my mother's silence, beyond my limited grappling,
my vision too narrow to fathom, even now, years later
in this room.

Miró's Landscape

Lunarscape, the echo
we long for — there is no night
like this, the yellow lip
quivers, rocks, the face as it
faces the dark side of the moon
looks away, moves
its belly on red sand
ready to take whatever the day
on this given ground delivers.

And hope, the buttercup shine
of a baby-eyelid
smacks its petal-lips in spite
of hard-line horizon
between earth and sky —
the moon, like an egg,
tips in the indigo:
alone the flower-faced spirit
knows nothing.

Clown

A smile, crazy with shame,
little lost diamond-eyes
the clown mask pushed
its face against the glass
days of empty rooms
when we played a mad tune
flippy with pigtails and mama's red lipstick
stolen for sheer revenge —

turned itself tight, yes,
little monster found its power
but got trapped in the smile
like a puppet, got locked
in the cold room,
wild at the boar-shaped world —

elsewhere it knew there was sun
like the ball left in the corner,
yellow as light of windows.

Glad Family II

I watched and (thought i) knew —
a grey winter afternoon:
           the fire in the iron hearth — my mother
emblematic in the green chair — she seemed
           to have fallen, drained out of herself,
           empty as if she would not re-fill
           the way i wished she would —
                     like the green glass vessels
                     circling on the metal wheel,
                     of the bottle-washing machine
                     in dad's old fruit-squash factory,
                     clear bottles transparent as light —
or like her face when she looked out at the garden
from the north-facing window-seat,
or the smell of biscuits baking
(i remember this) —
                     yet times like this, as if turned inwards:
           it seemed as if the rusted cans kept
           in the dark store-room cupboard
 had been placed there for us
           to find our way and somehow fill:
           like sharp-edged memories
           stacked on wooden shelves,
           they'd rub beneath our ribcages —
and dusted with flakes of paint
we stayed rust-bitten and itching.

The Well

Isaac

I could smell lime-dust in the wadi
that third night of our journey, stars were fading
it was cold. When sacrifice is called
blood spills in the sand, fur flies –

my father carried the fire stone
tenderly like a child, knife sheathed at his side.
But where was the animal
the offering?

With eyes turned deep he said
'God will see to it', and I believed.
We built the pyre, a tent of branches
each movement of our hands was ritual,

we had done this before, many times,
I followed my father, each move – then he
pulled me suddenly downwards, beard to my cheek
binding my ankles and shoulders.

My body water, his knife in moonlight,
my skin turned fur, breath dry,
dawn dashed across the sky
I could not hold its light –

then, as if for the first time, he saw
the other – ram in the thicket
curling horns, nostrils flared
caught in thorns. We could smell the blood.

I have seen my father blind
to the pulse beneath my skin —
his task great as stars in heaven
numerous as grains of sand on the shore

on this salt earth —
not seeing the sky, nor the child
whose heart beat like a bird
against the corner of a stone.

Abraham

Before that driest journey
I thought my feet were planted on rock,
had sunk a well, softened with Tamarisk
at the desert place Beer-Sheba.

Each day the skies breathed light on us
the Tamarisk pushed roots into salt
where I had written her name

we claimed her water in skin bags with silver spigots,
but some days I could not see my face
in the cold surface.

> After that night
> Isaac did not meet
> my eye a long time. Now
> I plead with him — say

> our lives are grasses in the wind,
> I have grieved each day upon the rock:
> this is all we have, beneath the Tamarisk, one star.

It was love that drove my hands,
the darkness between the stars
our seed time on this earth.

I might have used the blade,
the greater choice
to submit to the wind.

II.

In Forster (Sand up the Coast)

Pelicans motionless
      against the blue sky
mirrored in lagoons,
      or high up
      their wings
held by the constant wind –
a place so windblown, strange
to an immigrant: I stood
      on the beach
      as if I'd left
      my other wing
in another place –

not here, where the wind forces
the trees to lean
      downwards
and pandanus rough in the sand
has roots like legs pushed in
      against the sliding –

and I think of Eliza Fraser
      in her fringe of leaves
on an island of sand,
alien, harsh as salt
      and beautiful
the pools of water filtered clean
      through the grains –

how she had no choosing,
had to find in the straps
of the leaf bracts,
      learn how to seek out
the toughness

and her feet scratched and bare
were pushing down,
      sucked into sand
      as the wind blew
      her green and leathery.

A Book

I'm leaning towards a book
with pages the colour of honey
and linen – as if clawed
from a desert wadi cave, preserved
by cold arid nights:
threaded like beads on fibres of jute
the words in this book
veil a quiet love – hidden
in the traces of names of things
I want to hand to you: feather, wood,
a whitened shard of glass smoothed by tides,
grains of sand sieved fine through my fingers,
the chambers of a nautilus.
Can these objects – stone, pebble, driftwood, shell –
echo my body's sound waves
transmitting like whale-song
or a pulsing satellite arcing across the sky?
A body in feeling is silenced
in face of wind-tunnels of distance –
only the emptiness in my hands
is the name of my love – a blown
feather, a multiplication of cells,
a book without end,
amber pages and caught threads.

Chinese Box in Hong Kong

Roots of a banyan have taken the stone wall,
this street is uneven, threatens ankle-twist,
the air thick with heat, humid with fumes –
bloomers and t-shirts hang above the canopy
of a restaurant, modern food in lacquer bowls,
shiny shops, heavy jade buddhas – money runs
in the veins of this city, in drains of wet markets –
and fancy boys in pants cut for tight hips
and haircut perfection queue for noodles, the best in Soho
where sidewalks slide down hills, the escalator clacks
up to Mid-Levels. I buy red happiness candles
and an antique box of leather, also red,
its dark metal yin-yang clasp a promise –
one day I will learn this can be home,
that you thrive like scarlet bauhinia
growing on rocky peaks of this city
with its dumpling stalls and teeming streets –
its speed the energy
in the tips of your newest roots.

Flying Fox Poem

Like a flying fox tuned to airwaves
circling solitary and off-beam,
pressing its own horizon line
tiny-heart sensing the current –

I remember the wasp-sting
on your brow, cry of outrage fright-
filled at two – I could
lift you then, encircled,
a yolk inside a fragile shell:

how to blunt a needle –
resonant my ear of tin
reads and misreads
vibration as wasp-sting –
crack, and crack again
the albumen membrane
shellacked to my horizons:

you fly: the invisible remnant casing
a disintegrating broken sound –
fragile eyelid marks my fingertip,
pieces of shell, sand in my mouth.

Salt

Greek olives taste
intense as salt crust around a dry lake,

edge-of-the-tongue words
want nothing but to carve

the face on which not even love
nor the losing of love

nor the bite of a sensual afternoon
will salve the bitter line, the sting on the tongue:

rather than wrestling for words, were I
to paint this table with a brush in this hand

I wonder, would your absence fold over
and move a more tangible language

for a throat hard-wired,
a bow-string wanting

mouthfuls of clear water
in a dry cicada strip of afternoon?

Drought Poem

Gullies cut through rock, collecting damp,
the cool shadows wait for rain
through hot dust of seasons,
spinifex, ash – then, feathered fronds
spring from spores patient as stones,
grab shards of light, atoms of water
in night crevices of rock, take root
away from scorch, crack of leaf and clay.

Trees that have died here are crucifixes
witnesses to country
too hot and dry, their bark bone-white or burnt
black, brittle arms angle to the sky
or lean to the ground, derelict against the wind,
the shadow-ripped hills and sacrificed spaces.

Hill with road – on Arthur Boyd

Driving the red dust road
in forest near Balingup late winter,
eucalyptus and yellow wattle like pollen
stud slopes on the high side,
redgum trunks holding the valley,
whitened trees reaching limbs to the light,
whoop of whip bird, crackle of leaves –
air motionless as breathing ants,
sky clear as water, the azure blue
as a still moment – knowing the valley
will close over with its quiet
ticking after we have passed.

What next?

What comes next —
an image or a tool
I pick up, not knowing
the word to come:
a red board, a blue page,
that figure, this moment
after what has gone before: dregs
of yesterday then it's morning —
what next: a pulse
a blink, nothing you'd notice —
but there's the white window
you don't turn to, the light pane
a mirror at your shoulder,
a deliberate bend of offering,
a refusal to step into the next
hour or day, to fail
each time it passes — or
stifle the rush, clench
knuckles to lips, then catch
in the corner of an eye
the bend of an arm,
the angle of your face
to the wall.

The Pier

A finger in the dark
the pier ramped out
its planked goodbye:

the sea black as the night
behind us, lights sprinkled
the horizon, we walked out

to moonlight obscure
with translucent clouds:
no telling – but I could –

this was a casting out, not a beckoning,
palm trees picked up the wind chill
the shiver of never again.

Beneath rotting palings,
slide of tides and sand drift,
barnacles clamped tight their hard
grey shells – their pulsing muscle.

Alleys

Like spaces between poems,
cracked concrete yards between buildings
where weeds grow, are pitching for sunlight:

words creep
like rats, they scuttle the bins
and bottles of the night –

the back-lanes, if you go there
are sometimes soft as closed eyelids, blind faced
houses turned to the street: in the unlit night

the screeching of anarchic cats, a child crying,
a voice from somewhere could be of pleasure
or anguish. At dawn, exhausted fences lean inwards,

over palings where fruit-tree branches hang, dry
thick-skinned lemons, sun-hardened, bird-picked.
Wind gusts drift papers and grit into corners.

On a back step, a pot of scarlet
bougainvillea – the pavement gives way
to soft purple flowers of clover

their intimacy
of an inner wrist exposed
by a dressing-gown sleeve pushed

back from wet soapsuds in a sink:
back in alleys there's a thrumming, like heartbeats –
it thuds and blossoms and roars.

White Lines III

i
as from great height, look down on how we run
striving, awkward parallels
the messiness of crossings
like rain-soaked roads where
mud never dries – my feet

suddenly light with shock:
over and over each life
losing itself.

we are wet and pure, our naked arms
expose themselves again
like leaves after rain
intensely yellow with gloss

as if we are weaving a nest and the yellow shapes
gleam like pieces of foil amidst
sodden threads and grasses,
as if our eyes are everything
pushing through darkness

ant-like our paths manage
to climb past the rifts
of our losses: how to tell
in words not sound enough,
the crash of the inner pounding?

lines on a canvas, slashed – dried paint caught in a net of moment
                    in fiery thrust: if we had
                    no language nor sound
                    would we be brutish only
                    or still run the patterning earth
                    with irregular, broken
                    lace-work?

ii
in this night of silence
                    i cannot deny words unless
                    like a drying hibiscus flower
                    i am ready to fall – but nothing is arid

about this green coursing. the clouds passing the moon
                    tell me i will not be here always,
                    nor my feet on this muddy path footprinting
                    the wet grass: one day

sky and leaves will close over like doors to a veranda
                    moss on terrace stones
                    will change to white, then pink,
                    then green again with time –

the slow tongue-driven, thought-driven words attempt
                    to fill and deepen
                    eyes' bright windows –
                    a tentative dialogue.

White Lines II

for Jessie

in the gravel of a road
all that we have layers itself
at the pointed juncture
of this cold, white moment:
the brown earthy past is damp,
channelled as if tears
had whitened the start-stop beating:
I was hopeful for clarity,
for something clear as water
not this effort on and on –
the marks on a board, the clippings
on the wall, the loss steering
caulked silences of days –

something clear as a white line
floating, hopeful, across *this* second,
this pocketed clawed-for
little hunting self, seeking satisfaction

like letters of a name not written,
white-pointed footprints on air:
even the muddy cracks, spoors
you made, nose-driven
on suburban pavements mucked with litter,
sniffed absences of others:
the white lines passed each other
and they shone.

Obliquely

A hospital room, angled through a window
a tall apartment block outside, the plane tree
shifts from green to red to bare over days:
I look out – see, as if slanted ahead – a way tantalising
with mystery: high trees cast shade on either side,
the path moves coolly into the distance
then reaches a hill, dips to a winding
walkway between the trees
down beyond my sight line –

I wonder if the pathway enters woodland,
peaceful and hidden like an alley behind houses,
if it shows in local ordinances or maps.
I think when I leave this place
I will seek the ending of this passage, walk
this new revelation in my well-traversed suburb,
cleave its secret to my wholeness:
the quiet of dark leaves and cypresses,
promises like words, ink on a page –

then on a morning, something changes:
perception unfurling from a mangle
takes on a different turning, a flattening –
and the path to a vertiginous hill
is no longer a winding question,
nor potentially on a map – it is, I see
the long roof of a car port at the garden boundary
of the yellow brick apartments next door.
I start to notice people: a grey man in a raincoat,
a young man with a sports bag. Days
are afternoons, evenings: sleep and waking,

the bones of my skull mending to a knitted seam,
outside, the pebbled carport shelter
a perfect horizontal, a quotidian structure –

but the downward hill through the oblique window
shifts back and forth in ambiguity: a Rubin vase –
the ache of the real, a blow,
the leaves of waking dreams.

Feathered

The Art Gallery of NSW

Woolloomooloo framed through glass,
gallery colours run, a sky with feathered clouds
enters the room like an artwork.
Inside, a child sits upon a bench,
her skin translucent in the light.
The rain has stopped, a man in a raincoat
walks a path outside, his head bent:
the tears of the man in Martin Place
washed the city, the ordinary
unmasked howl, the beauty of human,
a rainbow. Behind each face
a washed china bowl,
tender diaphragms billow
like ceramic glaze, like underbellies of fish.
The child moves away, pigtails flipping:
sun breaks the grey harbour —
pylons and ships, a study of real-life:
like this, each painting beats its heart —
a heavy-lidded woman props an elbow
on a table, face turned inward,
Boyd's Adam and Eve fearful, naked
fleeing their bush paradise,
Nebuchadnezzar flames fire, burning
earth forges through genitals, hands:
each gesture is breath,
each knife-edged brushstroke or line
the defenceless eye,
a white-feathered bird's light shadow.

After the War

In his deepest dreams the ruined
city of Hamburg saw derelict bodies
stopped: the child was seeking
splinters of coal
        along the train tracks
for fire at home – to melt the fat
his mother collected from the sausage-works,
the way it caught on the rim of a bucket –
the taste still edges his tongue
        despite the sachertorte and coffee –

rumours of memory, a brown rust residue
stays in the cells of his bone and skin knowing –
even as lead-weight wings
struggled to propel the nights
        heavily into daylight –
he carried clumps of lead
in his pockets, walking into 1951 –

the rage to forget creating
clean-spun shining rebuilt cities,
old cobbles forged to new streets –
still, the leaded stones
pulled down on heart muscle
while his shoulder-blades fought
to lift – like the emerald-faced
wild geese over the river
their heavy bodies ascending:
and the lead-grey memories,
flints of coal imprinted
on frozen knees

still scraped the rough papers
of wintering skies.

The Names – photographs of August Sander

In each gelatin eye, the light – framed
images lock in categories – chairs, cupboards,
taxonomies of work – knives of a glasscutter,
tools of a blacksmith, carpenter, bureaucrat –
each likeness a hope cut clean:
1922, 1926 – the photographer's eye seeks variation –
the scarred, the maimed and blinded,
the poor and not employed,
earthbound woman, revolutionary man.

      I search amongst the faces –
middle-class wife, doctor, artist, student,
inhabiting tidy rooms and doorways,
intellectuals, gymnasts, architects –
      then, in 1938, 'Victims of persecution' –
categories begin to waiver – the names
ripple out from photographic surfaces:
      'Dr Phillips', 'Dr Kahn', 'Mrs Michel' –
disrupt the glassy portraits and Westerwald lakes
adjacent on the gallery wall, fan across time
as if turning over the dark undersides
of submerged rocks, unfold
from beneath the surfaces,
sunlit flashes, like knives,
like the silver bellies of the cold
fine-boned carp of the lakes.

Gold Miner's Hut, Hill End 1872

Soaring eucalypt frames the foreground
like a landscape by Constable or Corot —
steep valley walls enclose a cosy hut,
a fence of sticks erected,
smoking chimney, a rug airing on the picket —

but the ground here is unstable:
something has happened —
trees are stripped of their bark,
skins exposed out of season, broken
branches mess the valley floor, cut
or fallen from trees that are dying:
a man sits posed amongst broken, shattered rocks —

bend the frame of the picture's silence:
no birds call, no crickets rub their legs
shrill: only the racket and din
of the stamper battery crushing rock,
grinding quartz day and night
across the mill pond covered
with a stagnant film of shaking dust.

Yellow

The journalist Nat Gould gazes into a doorway of
a Sydney Opium Den 1896.

My pipe is honey, Englishman,
to you I am indolent yellow
on a low bed in my house of pleasure,
head on a silk cushion, hip rounded.
I see you clearly through the smoke
sweet odour of my O P'Ien,
my slender pipe of bamboo like a flute.
Your slack mouth hangs with lust —
is it my cheongsam body you desire
or the pagodas, ice and crocodiles
the Herb of Joy brings,
the fine pitch of taste, the way
my smooth skin lives?
You at the door, half in half out,
— I am not a woman
but opium and sex. You would steal it
as your country did at Nanking,
pious in your avarice.
My life is nothing to you —
I am dragon-woman
exotic as baboons and monkeys.
This is no den, it is your own
dark cell. Your necktie
is choking you. I am fierce as fire,
my hands are small —
yes, drink from your hip flask, Mister,
shake my gaze from your face
if you can.

Notes & Acknowledgements

Poems in this volume were influenced by the following works:
'Their Soles': William Kentridge, *Tide Table* 2003; 'Poinsettias': Grace Cossington Smith, *Poinsettias* 1931; 'Glad Family II': Colin Lanceley, *Glad Family Picnic* 1961–1962; 'Miró's Landscape': Joan Miró *Landscape (Paysage)* 1927; 'Drought Poem': John R. Walker, *Gully and Dead Tree* 2005; 'White Lines II' and 'White Lines III': Tony Tuckson, *White lines (vertical) on ultramarine* 1970–1973; 'After the War': Anselm Kiefer, *Glaube, Hoffnung, Liebe* 1984–1986; 'Gold Miner's Hut, Hill End 1872' from Merlin and Bayliss, Holtermann Collection.

Poems in this collection appeared previously, some in slightly different form, in: *Antipodes, Axon: Creative Explorations, Cordite Poetry Review, Mascara Literary Review, Southerly, StylusLit, TEXT: Journal of Writing and Writing Programs, Transnational Literature, Westerly*, and *Newcastle Poetry Prize Anthology, 2021*.

www.ingramcontent.com/pod-product-compliance
Lightning Source LLC
Chambersburg PA
CBHW020907100426
42737CB00044B/710